Be Intentional Today

Be Intentional Today

TEN TRUTHS ABOUT MAKING THE MOST OF YOUR LIFE

Dick Biggs

All Scripture verses are from the Open Bible, New Living Translation (NLT).
ISBN-13: 9781540557780
ISBN-10: 1540557782
Library of Congress Control Number: 2016914972
CreateSpace Independent Publishing Platform
North Charleston, South Carolina

TO:

Darryl i Barbes

FROM:

Dick Biggs

DATE:

December 9, 2016

MESSAGE:

Thanks for your
friendship all
these years,

Dedication

"You only live once. But if you work
it right, once is enough."

—FRED ALLEN

This little book is dedicated to two special people in my life who
worked it right:

Miss Eloise Penn was my English teacher, newspaper
adviser and speech coach during my sophomore, junior
and senior years at East Atlanta High School in Atlanta,
Georgia (1960–63). Fortunately, this extraordinary woman
saw me for what I could become, not for what I was—an
underachieving, immature and directionless teenager
whose classroom grades and conduct were disgraceful
up through the ninth grade. My life changed dramatically
because this caring educator valued making a difference
more than making money. Thank you, Miss Penn, for your
passion, knowledge, thoughtfulness, patience and dedication to the noble profession of teaching.

Jack McDowell has been a good friend, master mentor and gift from God for more than two decades. Judy and I have experienced a myriad of successes and setbacks over our thirty-two-year marriage. Jack is the epitome of enthusiasm and encouragement. His inspiring letters have lifted us up when were down and sent us soaring when things were going well. We look forward to our periodic lunches. We value his wisdom. We cherish his loyal friendship. In short, we appreciate him being there for us. This tribute is a small token of our boundless and abiding gratitude. God bless you, Jack, for your exemplary Christian example and influence.

Table Of Contents

Introduction

intentional: "deliberate...done with
full awareness...willful
...on purpose...conscious...planned...
by design...voluntary."

*L*ife is so incredibly short! Grandmother Eva Hall shared this wisdom with me when she was in her seventies, but her advice was beyond my youthful comprehension. Now, having lived more than seven decades, I understand fully what my maternal grandmother meant. God's gift to us is a finite number of days on this earth. The wise use of this precious time is our gift to God.

Yesterday is gone. Tomorrow isn't guaranteed. Today is all you have to be intentional about your destiny (what you become) and legacy (how others will view what you become).

You're either living intentionally or unintentionally. **Key question:** What will you do *today* to make a meaningful difference with your time, talents and treasure? This daily decision has crucial consequences for you and, believe it or not, everyone in your sphere of influence.

I learned the hard way about the swiftness of time. Alas, many of my youthful years were squandered and can never be recaptured. This unintentional part of my life was marked by a series of events from childhood until my thirty-seventh year:

- During my elementary and junior high school years, I made below-average grades and received poor conduct remarks for "talking too much in homeroom...being disruptive in class...annoying others."

- My parents divorced right after I graduated from high school. I went to college and didn't adjust well to campus life. I worked part-time as a waiter, served on the school newspaper, attended classes sporadically and dropped out after one semester.

- As a Marine sergeant, my last two years in the Corps were spent at the American embassies in Warsaw, Poland and Rome, Italy on the elite security guard program. It was a memorable experience with some remarkable leatherneck brothers, but I drank and partied excessively.

- Following my military discharge, I spent a year as an Associated Press staff writer before a thirteen-year stint in sales and sales management. While I did well financially and was physically fit, the rest of my life was unbalanced and woefully unintentional.

- I married in 1970 and was divorced less than three years later. Her unfaithfulness was the breaking point, but our union was probably doomed from the start because we had too many differences to overcome. In retrospect, I wasn't mature enough for matrimony.

- I spent nine tumultuous years as an unintentional bachelor. It was all about me, merriment, money and many hours at work. Eventually, I burned out spiritually, mentally and emotionally (see truth eight).

Fortunately, the most impactful turning point of my life occurred in 1982. On October 4, I launched my company with little cash ($2,000) and lots of enthusiasm. Business ownership provided the freedom to set my own schedule after working ridiculously long hours for others. I decided to work hard, but not all the time.

On December 15, I met Judy and we married nearly two years later. I returned to my Christian roots—a most welcome change—due to Judy's influence. Unquestionably, I'm a more intentional man thanks to my wife's godly example.

If you or people you know are following in my early footsteps, perhaps this book will be a rousing wake-up call. I'll be sharing ten truths about making the most of your life. Read each section carefully. Make a candid examination of how you're doing in each critical area. Complete the action plan at the end of the book.

Caution: These ideas only work if YOU do. It takes a burning sense of urgency to go beyond intentions to implementation. Otherwise, your excessive idealism will cause you to waste valuable time. Be a realist. Embrace intentionality as one of your virtues and make today count for something worthwhile.

Unintentional is defined as "accidental, inadvertent, aimless, negligent, thoughtless and careless." It's senseless and shortsighted to waste a single day living accidentally, inadvertently, aimlessly, negligently, thoughtlessly or carelessly. Your life matters. Be intentional today.

Dick Biggs
Gainesville, Georgia
October 2016

> "If I had five lives to live, I'd do a lot
> of different things. But when you have one
> life, you have to choose very carefully what you invest
> your life in. You want to make it count."
> —DANNY WUERFFEL, HEISMAN TROPHY WINNER,
> EXECUTIVE DIRECTOR OF DESIRE STREET MINISTRIES

TRUTH 1

Determine Where You Want To Spend Your Time

"The bad news is time flies. The good news is...you're the pilot."

—MICHAEL ALTHSULER

oday is going to depart and tomorrow is going to arrive no matter how you spend your time. So if you really think about it, what is required to live intentionally? You must be a serious student of time strategies and time tactics.

Time strategies deal with dominant interests or the areas where you live your life—family, place of worship, work, exercise and so forth. Like any strategy, it's a broader picture for how your life will unfold.

Time tactics pertain to how you divide up today among your dominant interests. Like any tactic, it's a targeted plan for pursuing and realizing your hopes and dreams in the important areas of your life.

Many years ago, I developed a simple graphic that enables me to clarify my long-term time strategies and concentrate on my short-term time tactics for today:

Dick's Dominant Interests

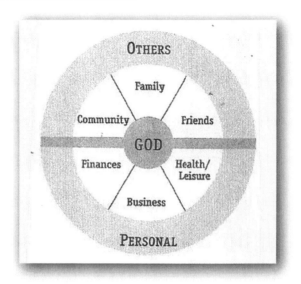

Before proceeding, understand two things. First, I'm not trying to dictate your dominant interests. Your chart may look very similar to mine or vastly different. If you're an atheist, obviously God isn't in your life. If you're unmarried, family isn't the same as someone with a spouse, children and grandchildren. If you're sedentary and overweight, healthy living may not be a major concern.

Second, this chart is perfectly symmetrical on paper, but not in real life. Each day is different and so are the demands on your time for certain dominant interests. You must decide today what's important in your life and how much time should be devoted to particular dominant interests.

My dominant interests were determined by using this outline— God, others and personal—in that order. **God** is in the center and, hopefully, flows out to my other dominant interests. **Others** are about family, friends and community. **Personal** is devoted to my business, finances and health/leisure.

Here's where I strive to spend time in my dominant interests:

God

This covers living my faith; having daily devotions; giving to my church and other charitable organizations; participating in Christian retreats and serving as a leader at my church; and striving to set a worthy example as a role model and mentor (truth two).

Others

- **Family**—This includes Judy, my wife; Rebecca Stvan and Tara Bryan, my stepdaughters; Bo Bryan, my son-in-law; Jackson Bryan, my grandson; Carol Johnson, my sister; Amy, Brandon and Riley Adams, my almost perfect niece and her husband and son respectively; Nikolas Frandsen, my nephew; Larry and Bev Askew, the son and daughter-in-law of Thurman Askew, my Mom's husband for thirty-seven years; Don Kreft, Thurman's son-in-law; and many in-laws.

  Daniel Biggs, my father, passed away in 2003. Bob, my brother, a decorated Vietnam Marine and the father of Nikolas in Denmark, died in 2006. Thelma Hall Askew, my mother, passed away in 2014. Thurman Askew passed away in 2015. Kay Kreft, Thurman's daughter and Don's wife, died in 2016.

- **Friends**—This is another special group of people besides family (truths three and four).

- **Community**—This has been dedicated to mentoring school kids in recent years (truth five).

Personal

- **Business**—This is about delivering keynotes and seminars on leadership, mentoring, teamwork and work/life balance; and developing resources that support my core topics (truth six).

- **Finances**—This includes the family budget, savings, investments, insurance, banking, tax and estate planning and so forth (truth seven).

- **Health/Leisure**—This encompasses my physical fitness program, proper diet and rest, regular medical and dental exams, vacations, entertainment and education (truth eight).

Ideally, you should have three to seven dominant interests. With less than three, you'll probably be out of balance. With more than seven, you're likely to be stressed out, even burned out.

Once you've decided on your dominant interests, understand that you'll spend more time in some areas than others. For example, I spend a lot more time on my business than exercising. I can't get my work done in three or four hours a week, but this amount of time produces big benefits in my health and fitness.

I spend a lot more time with family and friends than on community activities. However, mentoring Scotty Cole one hour a week from the first grade until his high-school graduation produced huge dividends for both of us. In short, every dominant interest requires a different time commitment.

Don't worry if a particular day is out of balance. There will be days when work is overwhelming. There will be days when you're tending to sick or dying loved ones. There will be days when you're on vacation. There will be days when you're volunteering in the community. There will be days when you're dealing with personal affairs. There will be days when you're enjoying some quiet time or fellowshipping at your place of worship.

Strive for weekly, monthly or perhaps quarterly balance depending on the particular dominant interest and what's happening in your life. If you're not spending the appropriate amount of time in these important areas, reassess how many dominant interests you have and what it will take to achieve a more harmonious lifestyle. It isn't a perfect process, but your life will be more fulfilling if you're highly intentional.

The next seven truths will reveal more about my dominant interests and why you might want to spend time in some or all of these areas. If you haven't thought carefully about your dominant interests, why not develop your own graphic? Please send it to me at dickbiggs@att.net, along with any comments about what you learned from this experience.

What you think, say and do daily determines what you become over your lifetime. It's never too late to change course. My desire is to inspire you to make the most of your life by being intentional today.

"Time" is a beautiful doo-wop song by the Dreamlovers. The lyrics include this stark warning: "Time goes quickly by...time waits for no one." Indeed, the clock is always ticking and the calendar pages are always turning.

Psalm 90:12 says it this way: "Teach us to make the most of our time, so that we may grow in wisdom." In other words, if you're not making today count, you're acting foolishly with the gift of life that God has graciously given to you.

You really are the pilot of your life, but a careful flight plan is needed to get you to the right destination. Be purposeful and laser-focused by determining what's really important in your life. Then, make the most of today by cherishing where you spend your time.

TRUTH 2

Place Your Faith In God, Not The Rat Race

"Do you know anyone who has ever
won the rat race?"
—Patrick Morley, *The Man In The Mirror*

Professional success and material possessions are worthwhile goals provided they don't dominate your life. But don't get so caught up in the unwinnable rat race of more stuff that you lose sight of *Who* makes it all possible. There's so much more to intentional living than your career and earthly belongings.

Even King Solomon, the wisest man who ever lived, discovered the futility of the rat race. He pursued power, pleasure, pride, prestige and possessions and eventually lamented: "But as I looked at everything I had worked so hard to accomplish, it was all so meaningless. It was like chasing the wind." (Ecclesiastes 2:11).

Not surprisingly, Solomon shared this mature advice near the end of his life: "Here is my final conclusion: Fear God and obey His commands, for this is the duty of every person. God will judge us for everything we do, including every secret thing, whether good or bad." (Ecclesiastes 12:13–14)

If you've read this far and you're a God-fearing person, you understand my way of thinking. Conversely, if you're an atheist or struggling to believe in God, you may be questioning my world view and tuning me out. I urge you to keep reading for this reason: **I believe it takes a lot more faith to reject God than it does to believe in a Divine Creator.**

If you doubt the Creation story found in the Bible, I understand your skepticism. It seems too supernatural to be true, doesn't it? For now, let's put aside the Bible and consider common sense. All of the material things we enjoy in life have a creator—homes, office buildings, restaurants, shopping malls, vehicles, cruise ships, airplanes, computers, televisions, smart phones and super highways with elaborate bridges and tunnels, to name a few.

It would be foolish to suggest these things just appeared out of thin air. All of these inventions have human creators. We don't doubt their existence because they're real and thus believable. We can see and touch them. We know they work because we've used them successfully. They make our lives more convenient and comfortable.

Now, let's consider the awesomeness of the universe and human race, which are far more intricate and impressive than any man-made inventions. Did our incredibly balanced universe just come together magically or did it have a Creator? Is the amazing miracle of childbirth just a fluke of nature or are we wonderfully made by a Creator? If everything else has a maker, doesn't it seem reasonable that the universe and humankind must have a Creator as well?

Following this line of logic, you may be thinking: I agree that everything we enjoy on this earth has a creator. But if God really exists, who created Him? It's a good question and serves as the ultimate test of faith when you read the Bible's first four words: "In the beginning God..." (Genesis 1:1) It implies the eternalness of God, a difficult concept to grasp with our finite minds.

Additionally, this may raise the following questions: Is the Bible reliable or merely a collection of ancient fables? Why should I believe in God when I'm not sure if the Bible is true?

First, there's ample evidence of the Bible's veracity, so you might want to do some extensive research and decide for yourself. Second, I urge you to read and study a clear translation of the Bible to learn more about God and why He can be trusted.

If you're still unconvinced about God and the Bible, here's what practical experience has taught me for more than seven decades. When I tried to live without God, there was a woeful lack of direction. Yet when God is in my life, I'm more purposeful, intentional and content.

Suggestion: Listen to *Who Needs God*, an enlightening five-part series by Andy Stanley. Go to northpointchurch.org and click on sermon archives.

Of course, having faith in God doesn't make me immune to problems and pain. I've experienced difficulties in every area of life and perhaps you have, too. The difference is that trusting in God has given me a "this too shall pass" attitude, making it possible to focus optimistically on the future instead of dwelling pessimistically on the past.

Best of all, God has given me the assurance of an eternal home in heaven, a place where "there will be no more death or sorrow or crying or pain. For the old world and its evils are gone forever." (Revelation 21:4)

If I've learned anything about faith, it's this: I don't have to know or understand everything about God to believe in Him. It's also true of many other things in life.

For instance, I can't explain how an airplane flies, but I've flown millions of miles. I don't know how a computer works, but I'm using one to write this book. I have no idea how engineers designed the Chesapeake Bay Bridge, including two long tunnels, over a twenty-one-mile span between Virginia and Maryland, but I've driven across it.

We've all heard of people who rejected God throughout their lives, only to seek Him on their deathbeds. Frankly, there's probably something in all of us that asks—at some point in time—is life on this earth all there is? Down deep inside, most of us believe God is around, especially in times of trouble. You probably can't count how often you or others have said, "Oh, my God!"

I spent nineteen years running from God because it seemed like such a relationship would require too much sacrifice. Looking back, it was the most unintentional season of my life for good reason. Like King Solomon, I was "chasing the wind" or, in modern terms, the rat race.

Faith in God makes my life more meaningful. Blaise Pascal, the seventeenth century French religious philosopher, put it this way in *Penses* when he introduced his wager: "You must wager; it is not optional. Let us weigh the gain and loss in wagering that God exists.

If you gain, you gain all; if you lose, you lose nothing. Wager then, without hesitation, that He exists."

So if God exists—and I believe He does—believers will "gain all" with the gift of eternal life and unbelievers will lose out on this promise. If it turns out that God doesn't exist, unbelievers won't care and believers will have lived more meaningful lives. This is a win-win wager I've gladly made—not out of fear, but out of respect for what God has done for me and many others.

Sadly, unbelievers often reject Pascal's direct message because it demands a lifestyle change and requires accountability for the consequences of immature choices and immoral conduct. Alas, in chasing the short-term pleasures of their earthly existence, they overlook the long-term treasures of a heavenly home. Compared to eternity, our lives are a mere tick of the clock.

Despite a desire to have a relationship with his children, God has granted us free will or the right to choose how we live without divine intervention. We can lead good lives filled with integrity, service to others and obedience to God's timeless truths.

Or we can enter the rat race and be damaged or destroyed by the abuse of money (greed), abuse of sex (lust) and abuse of power (pride). Be purposeful by using the gift of free will to cultivate a relationship with the eternal God of the universe instead of succumbing to such temporal earthly gods as greed, lust and pride.

To live more intentionally, decide where you want to spend your time—and then spend some of it with God, even though you'll never know or understand everything about Him. Your faith will cause you to fret less about past failures; face today knowing God is in control; and look to the future with anticipation, not anxiety.

If you're participating in the unwinnable rat race, do you want to discover, perhaps on your deathbed, that it was a misguided pursuit unworthy of your limited time on this earth? John Calvin put it bluntly: "The torture of a bad conscience is the hell of a living soul."

Most of all, do you really want to miss out on everything your Heavenly Father, through His son Jesus Christ, has promised (eternal life) and prepared (heaven) for those who believe in Him? If you haven't made this leap of faith, why not do so now? It's a decision you'll never regret and a bet you can't lose.

TRUTH 3

Cherish The Positive Influence Of Your Loved Ones

> "The foundation of civilization and
> human relationships is the family."
> —DR. LAURA SCHLESSINGER

J ust as there's no such thing as a perfectly intentional life, there's no such thing as a perfectly functional family. Truth be known, there's probably some sort of dysfunction in every family. Unlike friends, though, we don't choose our families; we're chosen, for better or worse.

It was a blessing to be raised in a strict family environment, but it was also quite stressful. My parents were busy Salvation Army officers who had four children in six years. We were loved. We were taught the difference between right and wrong. We were disciplined through spankings (force) and the promise of groundings (fear) when we behaved badly. Unfortunately, we also witnessed a lot of parental arguments and fights.

Our shaky family stability was devastated when Dan and Thelma Biggs divorced right after my high school graduation. As kids, we could have chosen to be victims of the family breakup, a situation beyond our control. Or, in spite of a difficult situation, we could have chosen to be victors by taking charge of our lives and moving on. I chose to be a victor.

I attended college for a semester, ran out of money and joined the US Marine Corps. I went on to success in three careers—journalism, sales and professional speaking and writing. Undoubtedly, these achievements would have been reduced significantly without the admirable qualities my imperfect parents instilled in their oldest child.

For example, my parents demonstrated the importance of promptness and why habitual lateness is selfish behavior that disrespects the time of others. They proved that orderliness saves time and produces greater efficiency. They encouraged me to be a lifelong learner and seek excellence in every endeavor.

My parents also taught me to focus on worthwhile goals and resist unimportant distractions. They showed me why a keen sense of urgency overcomes procrastination. Most of all, they believed there was no substitute for hard work and perseverance on the road to success.

A decade after my parents divorced, my first marriage ended in divorce as well. We never had children and I spent many years as an unintentional bachelor before meeting Judy. We married almost two years later and I inherited two stepdaughters, who were at the tender ages of fifteen and twelve.

It was a challenging time because Rebecca and Tara were dealing with the painful divorce of their parents and I was a clueless step-father struggling to fit into a blended family. Through the grace of

God and some tough love, we weathered the storm and the girls became responsible adults.

Rebecca Stvan resides in Houston, Texas, where she has a great job as an accountant at a real estate management company. Tara Bryan is married to Bo and they live in Acworth, Georgia with son Jackson, a high-school sophomore. Tara loves her job at a fleet-vehicle leasing company. Bo is a valued computer technician with a rapid transportation system.

While their biological father passed away in 2001, Rebecca and Tara now think of me a lot differently than they did when they were teenagers. Over the years, the girls have given me many touching cards and notes that validate my transition from stepfather to a father of sorts. I'm proud of them. I love them. And I'm confident they've learned some valuable life lessons from this old Marine sergeant.

Jackson is like the son I never had. Judy and I have spent many weekends, holidays and summers doing a lot of fun activities with our grandson. We've taken him on some memorable trips, including one to Washington, DC and Williamsburg and Charlottesville, Virginia. Judy and I have tried to build a long-term relationship with Jackson by doing the things he enjoys. We pray this influence will play a small part in our precious grandson living an intentional, purposeful and meaningful life.

Needless to say, this author's family hasn't been the ideal Ozzie and Harriett Nelson scenario of 1950s television. There have been some struggles and strife over the years. Yet, throughout these family trials and tribulations, I've realized it isn't healthy to dwell on what could have been. It's better to accept the way things are and look to the future with hope.

So whether you were raised in a stable or unstable family environment, here's the bottom line: You're in charge of your life. Learn from the good experiences and don't obsess over the bad ones. Above all, move on with the rest of your life no matter what family has been like for you.

> "One friend in a life is much, two are
> many, three are hardly possible."
> —HENRY BROOKS ADAMS, *THE EDUCATION OF*
> *HENRY ADAMS*

Along with family, friends can nurture a more intentional way of life. Conversely, choosing the wrong friends can lead to unnecessary tension, burnout and other unintended outcomes. Therefore, think carefully about the other significant people you share your life with.

There's a big difference between acquaintances (people you know) and friends (people you get to know). Having too many casual acquaintances can be time-consuming and cause unneeded stress. However, a select group of friends can make life more enjoyable and exciting.

Have you ever thought about what it takes to gain and maintain flourishing friendships? Here are five of the foremost factors that are absolutely necessary for these relationships to thrive:

- **Trust**. Nothing destroys a friendship like the lack of trust. Whether it's a marriage, business partnership or any other relationship, the foundation of a faithful friendship is integrity (being true to self) and honesty (being truthful with others). If you can't trust a friend, all else is suspect. Restoring broken trust is often as difficult as returning toothpaste to the tube.

- **Thoughtfulness.** Friends are givers, not takers. Friends know when to empathize and when to encourage. Friends think about love and loyalty, not gossip and self-gratification. Friends forgive, but they don't allow someone, including family members, to take advantage of them through a prolonged pattern of immature behavior and an unwillingness to change for the better.

- **Two-Way Communication.** A true friendship shouldn't be reliant on one person keeping the association vibrant and healthy. Just as it takes two to tango, proactive friends should make a mutual effort to cultivate their relationships. When this happens, both parties feel respected and resentment doesn't fester due to a one-sided situation.

- **Tenets Above Tolerance.** In cultivating friendships, tenets should trump tolerance. You can respect a friend's different habits, background, world view and so forth without compromising your core beliefs for the sake of acceptance and political correctness. When friends are focused on their common interests, they tend to create meaningful, merry and memorable moments.

- **Time.** Yes, it's true that some friends connect immediately. However, there's no substitute for time in building genuine, lasting friendships. It often takes years to really know someone and develop that special bond. Beware: Longevity can damage a relationship when two friends get careless by making assumptions and taking each other for granted.

Never underestimate the value of friends. If you aren't cultivating meaningful, positive support groups, why wait? You'll be surrounded by encouragers. You'll benefit from an ideal environment for authentic accountability. Most of all, you'll grow at a deeper level.

Perhaps Ralph Waldo Emerson said it best: "A friend may well be reckoned the masterpiece of nature." This is exactly how I feel about Judy, my wife and best friend for thirty-two years and counting.

∽∾∾

Optional Reading: The Henry Brooks Adams quote about the difficulty in having more than two or three friends is interesting. There isn't one person (family excluded) whom I've maintained an active friendship with since childhood—perhaps because we moved four times during my formative years. Instead, I've had many friends over the various stages and ages of my life.

Since it might be boring to read a list of people you may not know, be hereby warned that what follows is an acknowledgement of certain friends over the years. So before you skip to the next chapter, why not make a list of the special people who've made your life more enjoyable?

Now, with apologies to anyone I've inadvertently omitted, here's my attempt to offer thanks to the following people:

- Jack and Peggy McDowell, our oldest and wisest friends. Jack appears in this book's dedication and has been married to Peggy, a delightful woman, for more than fifty years.

- The many Browns Bridge Church small groups we've belonged to since 2000, including these couples: Bob and Gail Clendenen, Bob and Lynda Connor, Cliff and Martha Darby, Manning and Donna Davis, Frank and Kathy Galati, Jim and Martha Lanier, Jim and Lesslie Little, Paul and Katherine Morris, Steve and Liz Naughton, Darryl and Babs Neidlinger, Kelly and Joy Parham, Steve and Barb Radford, C. L. and Sue Smith, Dave and Peggy Thorne, Don and Maryann Wexler, David and Lois Williams, Steve and Linda Wood.

  We've relished the camaraderie, love and accountability afforded by these special friendships. It's part of our intentional lifestyle.

- My Friday breakfast buddies: Bob Clendenen, Jim Lanier, Jim Little, Darryl Neidlinger, C. L. Smith, Wayne Whited and Steve Wood. It's reassuring to have a group of Christian brothers who are there for you no matter what's going on in your life.

- Bill and Lynne Davis, our former neighbors who used to watch our home when we were away and taught us how to play the game of Mexican train.

- The quarterly outings with four couples who lived in Judy's neighborhood before we met: Bob and Lynda Connor, Manning and Donna Davis, Ed and Gail Stentz and Danny and Margie Tompkins.

- My agent and field leader partners at a renowned insurance and financial services company that has been my biggest client since 1990. It would take several pages to list all of them, but they know who they are. Exception: Thank you, Scott Foster, for introducing me to this remarkable organization. You and Linda are cherished loyal friends.

- Dick Dillon and Julie Onstott are special leaders who hired me many years ago to facilitate my yearlong mentoring program at Lucent Technologies (now Alcatel-Lucent).

- Dave Dunaway, a longtime chum who now resides in western North Carolina with his wife, Jane. Dave and I meet periodically for breakfast in Clayton, Georgia, about halfway between our homes, and enjoy sharing old stories and learning about new happenings.

- Some of the speakers who've influenced my life: Terry Brock, John Cooper, Patricia Fripp, Ken Futch, Gene Griessman, Lou Heckler, Bill Lampton, John Maxwell, Linda Miles, Nido Qubein, Chick Waddell and Richard Weylman. Rest in peace, John Cooper.

- My Walk to Emmaus reunion dudes: Dr. Gary Willis, chiropractor extraordinaire who always makes my aches disappear; and Tommy Bragg, a passionate musician and hilarious guy. We enjoy a good meal every quarter and have a lot of fun. John McMillan and Charlie Munn, two other Emmaus pals, now live in Texas and Virginia, respectively.

- Some of the Bereans Sunday school class members who were an integral part of our lives for fifteen years: Phil and Cathy Clark, Roger and Charlotte Dreher, Dwight and Brenda Kees, Lee and Nancy Lovvorn, Rick and Pam Page, Leland and Colleen Swift and Fred and Beth Townsend. Alas, Leland Swift and Rick Page died way too soon.

- My fellow Chattahoochee Road Runners (CRR): Cofounders Ron Creasy and Ron Varner, plus charter members Frank Crane, Rod Spence, Dwight and Brenda Kees, Fox and Kelly Ferrel and the late David Murray. We spent many hours helping CRR become Georgia's second-biggest running club. Even though Linda Crane and Marilyn Spence weren't runners, they attended our activities, along with Sharon Creasy, Ron's wife.

- My Marine brothers: Pete Jaynes, who was responsible for my enlistment in the Corps and is the one who accompanied me to boot camp and combat training; Ken Tapp, a former roommate and coworker; Art Lane, a special real-estate broker; Roy Lantz, a fellow speaker; Robert Sutter and Mike Boyce, two more Emmaus pals; and Bob Hollenbaugh, Bob Lenneman, Tony Ranallo, Al Rupich and J. D. Taylor, my fellow security guards at the American embassies in Warsaw, Poland, and/or Rome, Italy. Semper Fi, leathernecks!

- My East Atlanta High School classmates who helped make my transition from adolescence to adulthood a memorable time. There were only sixty-eight students in the class of 1963, but we look forward to our reunions every five years when we remember and relish those wonderful high school days.

- The countless Salvation Army kids who influenced my youthful walk with God and spiritual growth through worship, Bible study, brass band performances and summer camps. I'm thankful for this solid Christian foundation, which made it easier to return to after a nineteen-year absence.

TRUTH 4

Become A Connoisseur Of Caring Master Mentors

> "Mentoring is a developmental process, which means
> that you are constantly going to be on a learning curve."
> —HOWARD AND WILLIAM HENDRICKS,
> AS IRON SHARPENS IRON

One of the best ways to maintain a more intentional lifestyle is to seek wise counsel. More experienced people (mentors) are often eager to help you (protégé) avoid the mistakes they've made. In essence, a mentor is a special breed of friend dedicated to helping you reach your full potential.

Mentoring is one-on-one leadership or the pairing up of a less experienced person with a more seasoned person. It's a way to take role modeling to the next level. Mentors share life lessons with their protégés and, in the process, reveal who they *are*, how they *think*, what they've *done* and why they *have* something worth pursuing.

Anyone with more experience than someone else can be a mentor, but a master mentor *makes* the time to get involved in your life. Master mentors should strive to adhere to the following four benchmarks:

- **Master mentors "pursue what is true"** by focusing on these key questions: What do I believe? Why am I here? Where am I going?

- **Master mentors "turn creeds into deeds"** by focusing on these key questions: What will I do today? What have I done today? What will I keep doing tomorrow?

- **Master mentors "use congruence to influence"** by focusing on these key questions: Who am I treasuring? Who am I teaching? Who am I transforming?

- **Master mentors "collect a deep respect"** by focusing on these key questions: What about my lifestyle? What about my leadership? What about my legacy?

A master mentor goes beyond setting a good example to becoming "a trusted counselor, guide, tutor or coach." A master mentor says: *Here's a way to live that you might want to emulate...and let me share the details of my journey.*

As a proactive protégé, you should become a connoisseur of master mentors to shorten your learning curve and accelerate your growth. Here are four questions to ponder in observing your master mentors:

- **Do they *maintain* the highest ethical standards?**

- **Do they *sustain* a spirit of servant leadership?**

- **Do they *remain* true to their Creator?**

- **What memories would you *retain* if they died today?**

For years during my keynotes and seminars, I'd tell stirring stories about how master mentors had influenced my life. People would come up afterward and ask: *Do you have a mentoring program? We tried one at our organization and it bombed.* When I'd ask why, the answer would usually be: *Well, we paired up protégés and mentors and let them do their own thing.*

The tendency is for protégés and mentors to wing it in unstructured mentoring programs. This can be a recipe for failure, particularly when there's no action plan or measurable results. It's why I created *Maximize Your Moments With The Masters*, a yearlong mentoring program that features content, structure, flexibility, action and accountability.

Proactive protégés deserve a specific, structured track to run on, but want the flexibility to proceed at their own pace. They want to be challenged to take action. They want to be held accountable. This happens when master mentors are prepared, purposeful and passionate in helping their proactive protégés grow personally and professionally.

One of the greatest master mentors ever was the late Coach John Wooden, who led UCLA to ten national collegiate men's basketball championships—including seven in a row. In *Wooden On Leadership*, he makes this provocative statement: "I am unaware of any great team builders who were not also great teachers [read: mentors]."

I'm so grateful for the team of great master mentors who've poured their hearts and souls into my life. In turn, I've felt obligated to pass on their teachings to my proactive protégés. Think of it as a relay race in which the baton of wisdom and experience is passed on to future generations.

I'm a professional speaker and author thanks to a very special master mentor. As mentioned in the dedication, Miss Eloise Penn was my English teacher, newspaper adviser and speech coach for three years at East Atlanta High School in Atlanta, Georgia. Like all good master mentors, Miss Penn saw me for what I could become, not for what I was—an immature, underachieving and direction-less teenager with subpar grades due to lackluster application.

By my senior year, I was an "A" student in English; school newspaper editor; winner of some Optimist Club speech contests; recipient of the "Atlanta Quarterback Club Award" for outstanding athletic and academic achievement; and class graduation speaker.

This story isn't shared to boast about my accomplishments, but rather to honor Miss Penn for directing my educational path. There's no way I could have enjoyed a speaking and writing career for more than three decades without the dedicated mentoring of Miss Penn. She made a major difference in my life as a voice of encouragement. I'm eternally grateful for the gift Miss Penn so willingly gave to that lost teenager in the early 1960s.

In addition to Miss Penn, I hereby salute these master mentors: Dr. Michael Guido, Jack McDowell, John Maxwell, Lamar Matthews, Andy Hillman, Earl Masters, Linda Miles, Scott Foster and Staff

Sergeant W. A. McLain, my senior drill instructor during US Marine Corps boot camp at Parris Island, South Carolina.

I've tried to express my gratitude to these special men and women by passing on the life lessons they taught me. Besides several mentoring relationships I've had with professional peers over the years, I'm especially proud of two protégés: Scotty Cole, a former student in my community, and Jackson Bryan, my grandson.

Scotty and I met when he was a first grader. The school counselor said, "Scotty is a very sweet boy, but he needs to work on his self-confidence." A plan was devised to help Scotty become more confident. This exchange occurred during our one hour together at the school each week:

> **Dick:** What are goals?
> **Scotty:** Goals are things you want to do and places you want to go.
> **Dick:** That's right. And what is confidence?
> **Scotty:** Confidence means you can do something.
> **Dick:** And what will negative people tell you?
> **Scotty:** They'll say I can't do it.
> **Dick:** So what do you say to these people?
> **Scotty:** I CAN do it—unless it's something stupid or bad!

Every September, we established three goals at school and three goals at home. We repeated this format year after year. I monitored the progress of his goals, and we celebrated when Scotty succeeded in reaching them. When he failed to reach a certain goal, we talked about what could be done to make him successful.

One of my proudest moments was watching this young man graduate from high school in 2012. He wasn't an honor student, but the kid didn't quit and received his diploma. Best of all, Scotty stayed out of trouble during his school years by choosing his friends wisely. I haven't heard from Scotty lately, but I'm hoping he'll reconnect and share how his life is going.

Concerning Jackson, I participated in his middle school's "Watchdog" program for grandfathers from the sixth through the eighth grades. I spent many days attending Jackson's classes and participating in his studies. He looked forward to my periodic visits each school year and, of course, I enjoyed this special time with my grandson.

Since Jackson was a little boy, I've taught him something shared often with Scotty and elaborated upon in *Wisdom Gold*, one of my other books. I'm referring to the **4Cs,** which Jackson can recite on demand. I pray that these tenets will serve him well throughout his life:

- **Character** (or the lack of it) influences choices.

- **Choices** determine conduct.

- **Conduct** produces consequences.

- **Consequences** are a reflection of character (or the lack of it), choices and conduct.

If you haven't done so already, I challenge you to amass a team of proactive protégés. You have so much to *give* to less experienced people. If you don't have a team of master mentors, I urge you to assemble one. You have so much to *gain* from more experienced people.

Maybe Ken Blanchard had mentoring in mind with this statement: "None of us is as smart as all of us." It's the essence of one-on-one leadership as proactive protégés seek to learn and master mentors grow through teaching. It's a smart way to *add* intentionality to your life and *multiply* your influence with the people who'll pass on the relay baton of wisdom and experience to their successors.

TRUTH 5

Practice Servant Leadership In Your Community

> "Our leadership flows out of servant-hood;
> our first and primary
> drive is to serve, and our desire to serve
> motivates us to lead."
> —RICHARD J. FOSTER, *MONEY, SEX AND POWER*

The late Dr. Michael Guido, a great servant leader, was a master mentor to Judy and me for twenty years. As the founder of the Guido Evangelistic Association (GEA) in Metter, Georgia, he led this organization for fifty years. Dr. Guido epitomized servant leadership because he was the ultimate giver. He was also the most intentional person we've ever known.

Dr. Guido lived a full life at the Guido Gardens in southeastern Georgia. This beautiful three-acre paradise included his home, office building and a perfect place for a walk. He could be anywhere in this small town within minutes.

Audrey, his late wife, managed GEA's small team of employees. They never had children and were rarely apart. His idea of a "vacation" was when a board member flew him to churches across Georgia and elsewhere to deliver sermons.

As a result of his distinctive lifestyle, Dr. Guido practiced servant leadership at the highest level. He wasn't as famous as evangelist Billy Graham, but his influence within the Christian community was enormous. Dr. Guido shared his life-changing messages with millions of people around the world through devotional booklets, radio and television broadcasts, sermons and *Seeds From The Sower*, a wonderful book.

What made Dr. Guido really unique was his big heart. He made time for people, even when they'd pop in unexpectedly. He was a gracious host. He was a keen listener. He made you feel special. He always wanted to know what was going on in your life.

It was a chore to get Dr. Guido to talk about himself. We were honored to spend time with this humble servant leader. Judy and I made the eight-hour roundtrip drive to Metter numerous times. We have many fond memories of these visits and miss our dear friend.

Dr. Guido passed away on February 21, 2009 at the age of ninety-four. We were among the more than fifteen hundred people who attended his funeral. Shortly after his death, I compiled an album containing the many encouraging letters he'd written to us over the years. In the front of this album is a single page entitled "Some Favorite Michael Guido Memories." They include

- driving over the "Michael Guido Bridge" at exit 104 on I-16,

- admiring the Metter water tower that bears his moniker: "The Sower,"

- enjoying a delicious meal with him at Jo-Max BBQ,

- appreciating the power and passion of his precious prayers,

- witnessing such incredible faith and trust in God to supply his every need,

- marveling at his uncanny ability to focus on others and their needs,

- observing his remarkable humility and how he gave all the credit to God,

- reading his daily devotionals—short, relevant and so inspiring,

- sharing many of his insightful quotes in my programs and resources and

- looking at a photograph of us displayed proudly in my office.

Most of us will never measure up to Dr. Guido as a servant leader. Nevertheless, we should aspire to his high standard of service, get involved in our communities and make the most of our God-given abilities. In serving others, Dr. Guido believed in execution, not excuses. He said: "We must not wait until tomorrow to do what we must do today. Tomorrow may never come."

Here's what this great man taught me about servant leaders. They encompass all of the following characteristics:

- **Sincere**—Servant leaders are genuinely concerned about making a difference in the lives of others. They serve out of a sense of duty, not because they're looking for material gain or recognition. They have pure intentions.

- **Sacrificial**—Servant leaders forgo many short-term pleasures to help others cope with the long-term pain of bad choices, conduct and consequences. In selfless surrender, they're rewarded with true joy.

- **Sympathetic**—Servant leaders have a knack for understanding the plight of others. Perhaps it's because they've also experienced difficult times, and someone was there to ease their pain.

- **Secure**—Servant leaders believe in themselves. They know why they're called to help others. They don't think too highly of themselves lest it hinder their altruistic efforts.

- **Submissive**—Servant leaders are humble enough to acknowledge that God created us for a life far greater than self-gratification. They prefer to work behind the scenes and let their actions do the talking. They love it when others get the credit.

Browns Bridge Church (BBC), where Judy and I worship, is full of servant leaders. BBC is one of six church campuses that comprise North Point Ministries (NPM) in metropolitan Atlanta, Georgia. Elsewhere across America, there are more than thirty NPM strategic partners, which are independent churches that follow the model of the mother organization.

Founded by senior pastor Andy Stanley and others, some thirty thousand people attend the six metro Atlanta churches on Sundays. It takes hundreds of volunteers to make eighteen services possible—parking-lot attendants, ushers, audio/video technicians, musicians, adult group leaders and volunteers for all of the popular children's programs, to name a few.

If you were to interview these servant leaders, you'd probably hear these two comments: (1) Most of these people were reluctant to serve because of the demands on their time. (2) Once involved, they were blessed beyond anything imaginable. Yes, it really is in giving that we receive—a Biblical message that's as true today as when it was written centuries ago.

The opportunities for selfless service are unlimited, but you have to be courageous enough to take the first step and say yes. Proverbs 3:27 says it this way: "Do not withhold good from those who deserve it when it's in your power to help them." Now, in thinking about your community, whom and where are you serving?

Often people don't get involved in civic clubs, charities and churches, or they drop out of these organizations *because they're full of hypocrites.* Look, all organizations have some hypocrites because all of them are full of imperfect people. In a free society, the only behavior you can control is your own. Regardless of how others may behave, serve somewhere, honor your beliefs and practice what you preach because one person—YOU—can make a positive difference.

Sir Winston Churchill had a firm understanding of servant leadership when he said: "We make a living by what we get; we make a life by what we give." Unquestionably, professional success plays a vital role in the quest for a more intentional life. However, serving others produces a level of personal happiness that no amount of money and materialism can match.

Thank you, Dr. Guido, for your marvelous example of servant leadership. Will you strive to follow in his noble footsteps by serving somewhere in your community?

TRUTH 6

Choose A Captivating Career Over A Joyless Job

> "To be successful, the first thing to do
> is fall in love with your work."
>
> —SISTER MARY LAURETTA

P erhaps nothing can be more dominating than your career. It can trigger intense stress. It can lead to burnout and a most unintentional life. If you've ever dreaded going to work, you know how frustrating it can be and what a toll it can have on you mentally, physically, emotionally and spiritually.

Indeed, there's a big difference between a joyless job and a captivating career:

- A job is something you *have* to go to; a career is something you *want* to go to most every day.

- A job is something you often find boring; a career is something you find exciting and challenging most every day.

- A job is something that provides a livelihood; a career is something that will be a vital part of your legacy.

- A job is something you call work; a career is something that's fun most of the time.

- A job is something you usually can't wait to leave at the end of the day; a career is something you usually look forward to the next day.

- A job is something you yearn to retire from; a career is something that often makes retiring difficult to do.

- A job is something you fuss about frequently; a career is something you find fulfilling most of the time.

- A job is something you may leave because you're unhappy; a career is something you stay with because it's your life's passion.

- A job is something that often feels like an unwanted obligation; a career is something that feels like a wanted responsibility.

- A job is something you wouldn't wish on someone else; a career is something you encourage others to consider.

Retired people often say to me: *I had my job for forty years and hated it. I couldn't wait to retire!* Isn't this a sad way to spend half of your life? What if these people had replaced a joyless job with a captivating career? Perhaps they'd still be "working" today instead of grumbling about the miserable job they once tolerated.

I've loved words since Mr. Ray Skidmore, my sixth-grade teacher at Centre Street Elementary in Cumberland, Maryland, stressed vocabulary. On the first day of class, Mr. Skidmore wrote *miscellaneous* on the blackboard and asked if anyone could pronounce this word and say what it meant. No one could. Throughout that school year, a new word was on the blackboard each day.

My parents used to catch me reading late at night under the bedcovers with the aid of a flashlight. My love affair with words exploded when Miss Eloise Penn was my high-school English teacher, newspaper adviser and speech coach (see truth four). Diagramming sentences and writing term papers turned from drudgery to delight thanks to Miss Penn's teaching skills.

For more than three decades, I've had the privilege of informing and inspiring people with my keynotes, seminars and resources. It's truly a joy doing what I love to do. Retirement isn't something I've planned on, other than financially.

My captivating career has taken me to all fifty states and several foreign nations. I've met thousands of interesting people, stayed in hundreds of grand locations, seen scores of scenic sights and, hopefully, made a difference with my messages. It doesn't get any better than that.

Are there things about my career I dislike? Oh, yes. Airline flights get delayed or cancelled. Hotel and car rental reservations get botched occasionally. Meeting rooms aren't always ideal. Sometimes you get an audience that's had a rough night or just doesn't want to be there. The marketing is relentless. If there's no monthly production, there's no monthly salary.

Nevertheless, I wouldn't trade my career for anything else. I see it as a *vocatio*, which is Latin for "calling." I find it challenging, enjoyable and rewarding most of the time. Provided I'm healthy and audiences still want to hear my messages, I'll keep speaking and writing.

I tell young people that a high-paying career and happiness don't always go together. Of course, if they can make a lot of money doing what they love to do, that's a blessing and more power to them. You read in the introduction about my thirteen-year sales career. I was well paid and enjoyed building relationships with customers, but the long hours eventually took their toll and led to burnout.

Happily, this turning point was a catalyst for entrepreneurship, which has been a most interesting journey. On two occasions, I've had to make drastic shifts in my business due to market conditions beyond my control. There have been times when the cash wasn't flowing. Still, the joys of business ownership far outweigh any sorrows and setbacks.

Obviously, starting a business isn't for everyone. It's much better to work for someone else than be unemployed. Nevertheless, if you possess the following ten qualities, you're more likely to discover a captivating career whether you're an entrepreneur or employee:

Are you a creative thinker? Do you see the *general, idealistic vision* or "big picture" of where you want to go over your career? Are you setting *specific, realistic annual goals* to further your career? Are you *prioritizing daily* and working hard to make your dreams come true?

Are you optimistic? This doesn't mean you won't have some tough times in your career because you will. You shouldn't be oblivious to reality. However, a positive attitude should be your prevailing mind-set because, as Earl Nightingale said, "We become what we think about."

Are you trustworthy? Character counts in your dealings with coworkers, customers, vendors and anyone else you do business with. Long-term career success is never a certainty, but you'll surely fail if you don't set a worthy example by being true to yourself and truthful with others.

Are you self-motivated? The *external inspiration* of this book may stimulate your thinking, but it's your *internal self-motivation* that takes you from thinking to doing. While motivation by force and fear is often used with children, it rarely produces long-term results with mature adults.

Are you self-disciplined? This is the ability to change bad habits into good habits. Albert E. N. Gray wrote in *The Common Denominator Of Success*, a popular pamphlet, that self-discipline is "doing things that failures don't like to do" to get what you really want out of your career.

Are you a lifelong learner? Your career growth will be stymied if you're a know-it-all. Be a curious student who never stops learning about your profession, competition, customers and anything else that will make you more competent. Then apply what you know to generate results.

Are you decisive? Making hard choices can be agonizing. When facing major career decisions, ask: What will happen if I don't act? What are the possibilities if I do act? If for some reason I don't succeed, what's the worst that can happen—and can I deal with the consequences?

Are you a risk-taker? The late Robert E. Goizueta, former chairman and CEO of the Coca-Cola Company, said it well: "Remember, if you take risks, you may still fail. However, if you don't take risks, you will surely fail. More often than not, the greatest risk of all is to do nothing."

Are you resourceful? Things won't always go your way at work. When one door closes, look for another one to open. Creativity, commitment and courage, coupled with an ample dose of stubbornness and street smarts, will enable you to face adversity and persevere in your career.

Are you a doer? Ben Franklin said: "He who is good at making excuses is seldom good at anything else." You're either executing or making excuses. Which is it? Don't let procrastination or perfectionism sabotage your career growth. Do it NOW and leave a legitimate legacy!

Upon turning ninety, actress Betty White remarked in an interview: "Why should I retire when people keep asking me to do something I love to do?" I couldn't agree more. Refuse to let a joyless job lead you down that well-worn path of stress and burnout. Choose a captivating career, be more intentional and enjoy the journey for as long as you can.

TRUTH 7

Strive For Frugality And Generosity With Your Money

> "You must gain control over your money or
> the lack of it will forever control you."
>
> —DAVE RAMSEY, *TOTAL MONEY MAKEOVER*

Contrary to what some people say, money isn't the root of all evil. The truth is found in I Timothy 6:10: "For the *love* (emphasis added) of money is at the root of all kinds of evil. And some people, craving money, have wandered from the faith and pierced themselves with many sorrows."

Fact: There's nothing inherently wrong with money provided it's earned honestly, managed sensibly and used wisely.

Sadly, it's the overwhelming obsession with money that has destroyed the lives of many people and organizations. The relentless pursuit of money, with all of its material trappings, can be deceptive. Playing the "let's keep up with the Joneses" game can turn your life into a nightmare.

Parks Brown says it this way in *Jesus Or Money:* "Money can be a master if the heart places it before God. Keep a check on the level of your heart's true love for God versus the balance in your...bank accounts. Money battles with God Himself to be the master of your heart."

Growing up in the Salvation Army, my family never had much money, so frugality wasn't optional. Fortunately, Mom really knew how to stretch a dollar. When she'd send me to the neighborhood store to pick up a few items, Mom would say, "Now, son, don't buy anything that's not on the list." This wasn't a request; it was a requirement and life lesson on frugality.

I also learned about generosity as a youngster. The Salvation Army's noble purpose of serving others is made possible by the donations of caring people. I remember watching people drop money into a red kettle while I rang a bell at a crowded mall on a chilly day. It felt good to make the Christmas season a little brighter for folks struggling to make ends meet.

My father often told me about bagging groceries during the Great Depression of the 1930s. He earned a dollar per day and had to donate a dime of it to the church. Dad learned early on about generosity and undoubtedly it had a lot to do with him becoming a Salvation Army officer. He later started the charitable trust department for the Southern Territory of The Salvation Army.

Regrettably, I didn't practice these lessons on frugality and generosity early in my adult life. I spent unwisely for two decades. I became

a slave to debt. I saved sporadically. I didn't give to charitable organizations. My financial plan was nonexistent.

Eventually, I came to my senses and made some radical changes.
Judy and I live in a modest, mortgage-free home. We have one free
and clear automobile. We don't have any expensive "toys" that are
often purchased emotionally and used sparingly. We have a budget
and monitor it monthly.

We have one credit card and it's paid off monthly. We save money.
We're covered in the event of premature death, major medical
expenses and long-term care. And we're gladly giving to our church
and other benevolent organizations.

The good news about our thrifty lifestyle is that we have more
options. We don't have the stress of poor financial management,
which can have a major impact on other dominant interests (see
truth number one). We've been blessed with steady employment
for many years and have a comfortable retirement income. We give
freely, save regularly and live on the rest.

I wish these sound financial decisions had been made a lot earlier.
I could have saved more money, donated more money and been
spared a lot of agony. If you're reading these words and the rest of
your life is ahead of you, I implore you to embrace frugality and
generosity right now. It's a decision you'll never bemoan.

A major financial regret is cancelling two permanent life
insurance policies in my twenties. These policies had a fixed,
affordable premium and would now be paid up. The protection

would have always been there. The cash value would have been enormous.

Later in life, I had to purchase term life insurance because permanent life insurance premiums were unaffordable. Term provides much needed protection, but there's no cash-value benefit. Worst of all, the coverage often goes away in the golden years when premiums get too steep.

Insurance recommendation: Buy as much permanent life insurance as you can afford, as early as possible. Your economical premium will stay constant for the life of the policy and provide handy cash value. Later on, you won't have to worry about being uninsurable or rated in a high-risk/high-premium category due to a heart attack, stroke, cancer or some other debilitating health challenge. Best of all, the death benefit of your policy is passed tax-free to your beneficiaries.

Financial diversification: "Don't put all of your eggs in one basket" is a trite but true expression concerning investments. If your company has a 401K plan, participate at the maximal level as soon as possible. Contribute annually to an IRA. Check out an investment portfolio that includes stocks, mutual funds, bonds or precious metals. Buy a home and perhaps other real estate. Consider business ownership. Most of all, remember that if an investment sounds too good to be true, it probably is.

Monetary tip: With the exception of your home, do everything possible to avoid debt. Nothing will cramp your financial situation like excessive monthly payments. Remember, the only way money will make you happy is if you manage it properly.

Best investment: The late John Templeton was known as the "Dean of Global Investing." Moreover, hundreds of his clients became millionaires over many decades. When Mr. Templeton was asked to name the best investment he'd ever made, he probably shocked a lot of people by saying: "The most risk-free investment, the most rewarding investment, is tithing. It means giving ten percent of your income to the church and charities. I have never known anyone who regretted this investment."

Tithing is a Biblical principle. The temptation is often to keep as much for yourself and give away as little as possible. In reality, everything you have belongs to God. You're merely the steward of the bountiful riches placed in your care.

Stewardship is the wise management of what you've been entrusted with on this earth. A good steward is more concerned with the prudent *use* of money rather than its mere accumulation. Generosity, not greed, is the driving force behind this financial decision.

A good example of generosity is Jack Eckerd, who earned an honest living and made wise use of his profits as the founder of Eckerd Drug Stores. He donated millions of dollars to charitable causes such as Eckerd Family Youth Alternatives, a foundation that operates "wilderness camps" for troubled children; Eckerd College, previously known as Florida Presbyterian College; the Eckerd Foundation, which contracts with the state of Florida for the operation of a juvenile detention center; and PRIDE (Prison Rehabilitative Industries & Diversified Enterprises).

In *Eckerd: Finding The Right Prescription*, he says: "God has shown me, as I have prayed and read the Bible, that everything belongs to

Him and He expects me to make optimum use of it for the work He is doing in this world."

If you're having a hard time grasping the tithing and stewardship concepts, consider that no amount of wealth accumulation will be going with you at death—and would be worthless if it did. It reminds me of the Cadillac Ranch in Amarillo, Texas, where many luxury automobile classics are half-buried in a remote field with their distinctive tail fins pointed skyward. It's a strange, somewhat humorous reminder that we come into this life with nothing and we leave with nothing but our reputations.

Making money is important, but making a difference in the lives of others is a more dignified way to be remembered. A good way to serve humankind is to be more frugal so you can be more generous with your financial resources. This is probably what Ethel Percy Andrus meant when she shared this unique perspective on money: "What I spent is gone; what I kept, I lost; but what I gave away will be mine forever."

TRUTH 8

Manage Stress By Making Time For Serenity And Healthiness

"The first wealth is health."

—Ralph Waldo Emerson

f you've ever had a stress fracture in a leg bone, you know how painful it can be. When a bone is subjected to enough pressure, it develops a hairline crack. Your entire body is no different. If subjected to enough stress, it breaks down and can cause unnecessary pain and suffering.

Stress is your body's reaction to change, challenge, coercion or lack of control. It alters your equilibrium and can cause anxiety, depression, exhaustion, illness and even death. The Latin derivation for stress means to be "drawn tight" or, in today's lingo, to be "uptight."

Conversely, serenity is a state of peacefulness designed to relieve your tension. It's crucial to offset the unavoidable stresses of society with times of tranquility in the spiritual, mental, physical and emotional sides of your life. These stress relievers have helped me over the years:

- **Spiritually**—I try to make time each day for Bible reading, prayer and quiet time with God, but I don't always succeed. I read "Seeds From The Sower," a daily devotional from the Guido Evangelistic Association. Judy and I are small-group leaders at our church. I've served on fifteen *Walk To Emmaus* teams, a nondenominational, three-day Christian retreat.

- **Mentally**—I solve crossword puzzles most every day. I love playing Scrabble. I'm an avid reader and writer. I enjoy creating anagrams—the process of finding others words within a single word—as fun activities for my seminars. For example, there are at least one hundred and twenty other words within "teamwork!" I'm serious. How many of these other words can you find?

- **Physically**—I started running to get ready for Marine Corps boot camp in 1964. In my competitive years, I completed seven marathons, thirteen half-marathons and thirty Peachtree Road Races. Gradually, I cut back to running five days a week, then four and now three in my senior years. I run about fifteen weekly miles and work out on nautilus three days each week.

- **Emotionally**—Between Christmas and New Year's Day, Judy and I plan some of our tranquil times for the next twelve months: long weekend getaways, retreats, reunions, vacations and so forth. It gives us something to look forward to, which is a form of stress relief in itself. We also have solid support groups such as family, good friends, mentors and a church home.

In addition to these stress-relieving suggestions, be consistent in observing these "Eight Elite Enhancers Of Longer Life":

Get the proper amount of sleep and relaxation. Sleep is the body's way of restoring energy. Most people require six to eight hours of sleep per night. Without adequate rest, your body is more likely to break down, leading to a variety of health challenges.

Have regular, complete and preventive medical and dental examinations. Make sure your annual medical exams include cancer screening and stress testing. See your dentist at least semiannually. Remember, early prevention is a lot better than costly treatment.

Eat a balanced, sensible diet and maintain the proper weight. Consume a lot more good food than bad, including whole grains, fruits and vegetables. Drink a lot of water. To lose or maintain weight, here's a simple formula: eat less, exercise more and don't make excuses.

Exercise aerobically, reasonably and consistently. "Aerobic" means "with oxygen." Aerobic exercises include walking, hiking, running, swimming, rowing and biking. Moderation and steadiness are vital. If you're sedentary, get examined by your doctor before starting an aerobic exercise program.

Avoid all tobacco products. Some of the chemicals emitted from a burning cigarette include the following: benzene, a flammable liquid used in making dyes and rubbers; carbon monoxide, the same poisonous oxygen blocker ejected from a vehicle exhaust pipe; formaldehyde, a disinfectant and preservative; ammonia, a poisonous gas used in making fertilizers and explosives; and hydrogen cyanide, a poisonous rat killer. Enough said.

Say no to drugs and drink alcohol in moderation, if at all. Illegal drug use is just stupid. Excessive alcoholic consumption is expensive, damages vital organs, alters behavior, strains relationships and shortens life spans. Driving while drinking (or texting) endangers your life and the lives of innocent people, so be intentional and don't do it.

Use home smoke detectors and wear vehicle seat belts. Thousands of people die needlessly every year in their homes and vehicles because they overlook these life-saving devices.

Laugh often, particularly at yourself. It really is true that laughter is the best medicine. A good sense of humor is not only healthy, but it also makes you more fun to be around.

The reality is that you'll endure some stressful days and enjoy some serene times, but there's no such thing as a perfectly intentional life in an imperfect world.

First, *unintentional situations* will occur and are often out of your control. No matter how well things are going, the best of plans can go awry due to unemployment, increased workloads, illnesses, accidents, financial setbacks, divorces, loved ones passing away, natural disasters, wars and much more. These stressful situations can have a major impact on your quality of life.

Second, *intentional events* will often dominate your life for certain periods of time. For instance, when you're on vacation, your likely focus is relaxing for a few days. When you bring children into the world, your focus might be celebrating at home for a couple of weeks. When you start a business, your focus is probably getting the enterprise up and going for several months.

While these unintentional situations *and* intentional events are a part of life, you should strive for a reasonable measure of balance. Otherwise, you could suffer burnout, which is the extinguishing of your mental, physical, emotional and spiritual enthusiasm. To learn more, read *Burn Brightly Without Burning Out*, one of my other books.

Earlier in life, I paid a steep price for not following this advice and burnout hit me hard. I left a lucrative sales career in 1982 and didn't work for five months. It culminated in the turning point you read about in the introduction. I didn't realize then that burnout is optional!

Prior to this defining moment, I was driven by the *haves* of a materialistic world, a quest that influenced my *thinking* and *doing*. I failed to *be* true to myself, others and God. It was an unintentional lifestyle based on "have > think > do > be."

Since 1982, I've endeavored to live a more intentional life by *being* faithful to Biblical truths. This way of life has influenced my *thinking* and *doing*. My *haves* extend beyond material things to intangible blessings. It's a more intentional lifestyle based on "be > think > do > have."

I challenge you to answer these five probing questions in pursuit of greater intentionality:

- **Principles: Who am I? This is about your beliefs.**

- **Purpose: Why am I here? This is about your reason for being.**

- **Preparation: Where am I going? This is about goal setting and prioritizing.**

- **Performance: How will I get there? This is about goal getting.**

- **Perspective: When I get there, what will I have? This is about true success.**

In short, you live only once, so why not be as purposeful as possible? Take control of what you can. Let go of what you can't control. Above all, learn to manage stress by making time for serenity and healthiness to foster a more intentional and balanced lifestyle.

TRUTH 9

Understand Why Intentional Living Requires Liberty

> "I know not what course others may take;
> but as for me, give me liberty or give me death."
>
> —PATRICK HENRY

Warning: Everything you've read so far about the quest for intentional living is contingent upon one crucial word: *liberty*. People who "live" under tyrannical governments are frustrated and fearful. They can't choose their lifestyles because they're controlled by oppressive leaders who use force to maintain power and stifle individual freedom.

The American Founding Fathers had a passionate desire for liberty based upon Judeo-Christian values. Most of these men read and revered the Bible. They thought that no one, by nature, is the ruler of another. Instead, "the Laws of Nature and of Nature's God" provided the moral foundation and compass necessary for the American republic to survive and thrive.

Despite the prevailing and undeniable influence of Judeo-Christian beliefs upon early American society, the founders understood that freedom *of* religion—not freedom *from* religion—meant American citizens could choose their religious preference without fear of reprisal. Because these great American leaders had learned from history, they knew that liberty is lessened or lost when government and religion are one entity.

My last two years in the US Marine Corps were spent in radically different political environments. I served one-year tours of duty at the American embassies in Warsaw, Poland and Rome, Italy on the elite security-guard program. These diverse experiences taught me a lot about the natural longing for liberty by humankind around the world.

Poland was a communist nation in the 1960s. Stanley, a memorable embassy driver, used to define communism this way: "What's mine is mine; what's yours is also mine." The Polish government controlled virtually everything. Most Poles led discontented lives due to limited freedom under the "Iron Curtain."

In Warsaw, I saw Poles wait in long lines at the American embassy for a chance to immigrate to the United States. All they wanted was the opportunity to live in "the land of the free" and pursue the American dream. When accepted as legal immigrants, many Poles left their homeland with meager possessions and boundless optimism.

In Rome, it was refreshing to see Italians living free and making the most of it. Perhaps no people love life more than the gregarious Italians. It was a stark contrast between two vastly different ways of life—a free Italy versus communist Poland which, thankfully, is now a liberated land. I vowed to never take the many blessings of American liberty for granted.

In the American Declaration of Independence, Thomas Jefferson referred to "certain unalienable Rights...among them are Life, Liberty and the pursuit of Happiness." While these rights enable a free people the opportunity to pursue the American dream, they don't guarantee outcomes. Indeed, it's a privilege—not a right—to live in a country with such unlimited opportunity.

The US Constitution is the foundation of our remarkable republic. It's just as relevant today as it was when written and adapted in the late eighteenth century. Because it was crafted so fundamentally well, this guiding document has been amended only twenty-seven times in American history.

Hillsdale College, a champion of civil and religious liberty in Hillsdale, Michigan, requires its students to complete a course on the US Constitution in order to graduate. Now, thanks to some generous donors, you can take this superb ten-part course online for free. You'll learn a lot through the dynamic lectures. You'll take a multiple-choice quiz after each segment. You'll get a certificate upon completion. Plus, you can purchase an optional course companion book.

Go to info.hillsdale.edu and click on "online courses" to learn more. I urge you to enroll at once. You'll gain valuable insight into how the American republic was conceived. You'll discover how far America has strayed from its founding roots.

Capitalism isn't perfect due to periodic ups and downs, but it sure beats any other economic system. The American economy was in one of these down cycles when Ronald Reagan became president in 1981. It was a period of soaring inflation and high interest rates.

President Reagan concluded: "In the present crisis, government is not the solution to our problems; government is the problem."

President Reagan's bold economic policies led to incredible prosperity in the 1980s and beyond. This great leader knew that free enterprise works best when there's limited government, lower taxes and minimal regulation. Companies are more profitable and hire more people, who then enjoy a better quality of life. Companies are more confident when government provides the proper environment for capitalism to flourish and resists the urge to micromanage the business world.

America suffered another economic decline in the early twenty-first century—the worst since the Great Depression of the 1930s. Unemployment hit 10 percent. Massive entitlement programs such as Social Security, Medicare, Medicaid and the Affordable Care Act became unsustainable. The national debt topped $20 trillion and was climbing rapidly. Federal spending was out of control and most politicians were unwilling to embrace common sense and balance the budget.

President Reagan often alluded to America as a "shining city upon a hill." This lofty peak wasn't reached because of excessive government. It happened due to vast natural resources, innovation, industry and God-fearing people who valued freedom and opportunity. America can remain on such a pinnacle only when its citizens take charge of their lives and adamantly reject a "cradle-to-grave" government that erodes individual liberties. You should understand the following:

- **Freedom is definitely not free; the price tag is responsibility.**

- **Independence is dependent upon unwavering faith in God.**

- **Personal rights are wrong when they erode the moral fabric of society.**

- **Political correctness is incorrect conduct that sabotages authenticity.**

- **Diversity isn't enough to turn opportunities into outcomes.**

- **Time-tested tenets trump a tolerance that says all truth is relative.**

It's heartbreaking when people have their aspirations crushed due to circumstances beyond their control. High unemployment or underemployment is a dream killer for millions of Americans because it derails their "pursuits of happiness." Finances are ruined. Relationships are strained. Health often falters. Faith is sometimes questioned. Intentional living is turned upside down.

It's disgraceful when able-bodied people don't accept available employment. They'd rather survive with an entitlement mentality than thrive through an enterprising mind-set. They whine about their plights and often do nothing to better their conditions. Sadly, they're unintentional and proud of it.

It's remarkable to see so many *legal* immigrants choose hard work over handouts. Many of these people come from countries where freedom and opportunities are limited or nonexistent. They're grateful for the chance to succeed on their own merits without government dependence.

If you're lazy and expect a government bailout, shame on you. If you're unemployed through no fault of your own, stay positive, don't give up and believe that brighter days are ahead. If you're living the American dream and the lifestyle it affords, treasure the moment, count your many blessings and be humble.

The American free enterprise system is the envy of nations around the world. It's the reason people flee oppressive governments and rush to America's shores. They yearn to be free and live their dreams. When government doesn't abuse its power, there's absolutely no reason why every American shouldn't be able to enjoy "life, liberty and the pursuit of happiness."

Put another way, how can you pursue happiness to its fullest without liberty? And without liberty, coupled with responsibility, is your life really worth living? No doubt these were questions Patrick Henry pondered before proclaiming his famous words.

America's courageous Founding Fathers were willing to lose "our Lives, our Fortunes and our sacred Honor" for the sake of a free country. Therefore, we should cherish our precious liberties and live intentionally every day. Anything less is an unconscionable mockery of an *exceptional* heritage because there has never been another nation like the United States of America.

TRUTH 10

Decide Now To Leave A Legitimate Leadership Legacy

> "If you would not be forgotten as soon
> as you are dead and rotten,
> either write things worth reading or
> do things worth the writing."
> —BENJAMIN FRANKLIN

f you're wondering what your legacy has to do with intentional living, the answer is everything. The quality of your life will determine the quality of your legacy. The good news is that it's never too late to change your life and thus your legacy.

There are tangible and intangible legacies. A tangible legacy is something you leave to others in a will or trust agreement—money, real estate, stocks and so forth. An intangible legacy is how you'll be remembered after you're dead. Have you thought about how you'll be remembered?

Here's what a gentleman said after a seminar in which I'd talked about the importance of leaving a legitimate leadership legacy: *Why should I be concerned about my legacy? I might be remembered for a couple of generations, but then I'll be long gone and most likely forgotten. Why should I waste valuable time thinking about my legacy when it probably won't matter years later?*

Unfortunately, this guy didn't understand that a legacy—good or bad—is passed on from generation to generation even if specific names aren't recalled over time. Our words and ways are being watched by family, friends, neighbors, coworkers and even strangers. We don't always know how deeply we're affecting these people. Thus, it behooves us to care about our legacy because of the impact it will have on those who'll live on after we've passed away.

Alas, many people are so busy living their lives that they give little or no thought to how they'll be remembered. And while it's true that a legacy is something others may ponder once you've passed away, it's also true that your legacy will be determined by your character, choices, conduct and resulting consequences. For the sake of others, doesn't it deserve some serious thought while you still have the full capacity of your mind?

Tombstones often tell us a great deal about legacies. Judy and I have made several visits to Cades Cove, Tennessee, a beautiful spot nestled within the Great Smoky Mountains and about an hour's drive from Gatlinburg. There are some old church cemeteries in Cades Cove because this area was once inhabited by more than seven hundred people. One day, while reading the epitaphs on the headstones, this one caught our attention:

David W. Sparks (March 28, 1863–May 4, 1940)
He was a good father, husband and an honest man.

It's such a simple sentence, but it says a lot about this deceased fellow's legacy. Most likely, Mr. Sparks worked hard all his life in this remote area. He was born during the American Civil War and, having lived through the Great Depression, he certainly experienced some difficult times.

Yet, it appears Mr. Sparks made the most of his seventy-seven years by providing for his family and earning a trustworthy reputation within this rural community. While his gravestone doesn't say it, he was probably a man of God. After all, Mr. Sparks is buried in a church cemetery in the "Bible Belt."

Never forget that making money is about your livelihood, but making a difference is about your legacy. The most important legacy you can leave is your intangible spirit, which is passed on by how you live. This will have more long-term impact on your loved ones than any tangibles you transfer to them through a will or trust agreement.

Of course, there's nothing wrong with amassing great wealth as long as you don't sacrifice your reputation for riches. Money without morality often leads to greed. Money with morality often fosters generosity. Are you greedy or generous with your money?

The late Earl Masters, one of my master mentors for many years, left a significant legacy through his humble spirit. He earned a substantial income as a salesman and loved giving generously to his church and serving others. When Earl passed away on December 6, 1993, here's what one eulogist said about him:

- **He was true to himself.**

- **He was an encourager of others.**

- **He was a humble servant of God.**

- **He lives on after his death.**

To paraphrase: Earl lived with integrity, inspired others and influenced many people through his faith. Now Earl's immortality is not only evident through this tribute, but also through eternal life in his heavenly home.

Following Earl's death, I wanted to do something special to honor his legacy, but my efforts were coming up empty. About six months later, I was speaking at Amicalola Lodge in the scenic Blue Ridge Mountains of north Georgia. I had a free afternoon and decided to write a poetic tribute to Earl. It was a gorgeous day and these words flowed freely:

"When I've Passed Away, What Will They Say?"
by Dick Biggs

Did you lend a hand to someone today?
Did you touch a heart in a special way?
Did you give your best on this blessed earth?
Did you model the truth of your human worth?

Life's so fleeting it would be such a shame,
If you failed to honor your given name.
Set your standards high for others to follow,
Lead by example, lest your words ring hollow.

You're living your legacy, what will it be?
Is your life a beacon for all to see?
Did you seize each moment with full emotion?
Did you make a difference with firm devotion?

Don't squander time, there's much you can do
In the precious days God has given you.
May these words be your motto, this I pray:
"When I've passed away, what will they say?"

Your eulogy probably won't be determined by how you earned a living. Most likely, it will be based on the reputation you earned while living. Live with *integrity*. Be a source of *inspiration* to others. Let your *influence* be a reflection of your Creator. Have true *immortality*.

Proverbs 17:22 offers this wisdom: "A cheerful heart is good medicine, but a broken spirit saps a person's strength." Will you be intentional and live with a cheerful heart? Or will you be unintentional and perhaps be plagued by a broken spirit? Your quality of life hinges on this crucial choice.

Decide now to be fiercely intentional about the pursuit of lifetime significance. It requires being true to self, making wise daily choices and doing what's right in order to leave a legitimate leadership legacy. Now, what will they say when you've passed away?

CONCLUSION

*"Power is the capacity to translate intention
into reality and then sustain it."*
—WARREN BENNIS

The late Cavett Robert, founder of the National Speakers Association (NSA), was an intentional leader. He was told that NSA would never succeed because professional speakers would be unwilling to help their competition decrease the "speaking pie." Cavett replied, "We'll just build a bigger pie!"

When I attended my first NSA convention in 1986, I'd only been a member for four months. The only people I knew at this massive meeting were a couple of fellow Georgians. As an aspiring speaker, I felt intimidated and completely out of place.

After four days of listening to some of the best professional speakers in the world, it was quite apparent I had a long way to go. My head was spinning with a myriad of ideas and what needed to be done. Even though it was an exciting time, I was doubtful about attending another NSA convention because it had been such an overwhelming experience.

At the reception prior to the closing dinner and awards banquet, I was approached by an elderly gentleman who asked my opinion of the convention. "Well, sir, this is my first one and I'm in awe of what I've seen. However, I'm not sure if I'll ever be as good as the speakers who performed here."

Smiling, the compassionate old-timer said he understood my feelings and remarked: "Most every great speaker was once a bad speaker. It takes practice and a lot of experience to excel on the platform. You have to be really intentional if you want to succeed in the professional speaking business."

Then, this gracious man invited me to join him for dinner at his table. We entered the huge banquet hall and kept walking until we reached the center table at the front of the room. Turns out, my host was Cavett Robert, the NSA founder. It was a wonderful evening, one that changed my attitude about what it would take to excel on the platform.

A few days later, Cavett sent me a cassette tape (this was before CDs) entitled "The Five Bridges To Professional Speaking." It suggested that becoming an accomplished speaker would require dogged intentionality. Cavett's words led to the creation of the four Ms of my profession: *m*essage (topics), *m*essenger (spiritual, mental, physical and emotional preparation), *m*arketing (clients) and *m*anagement (administrative matters).

In a similar way, are you willing to be fully intentional in the pursuit of what you want out of life? In other words, do you have a clear purpose, passionate vision, specific goals and daily priorities to turn your dreams into a dignified destiny and get you to your desired destination? If not, today is the time to be intentional about your life! Don't procrastinate another day!

The late Dr. Charles Jarvis, a dentist who became one of the greatest humorists of the twentieth century, understood the perils of procrastination. In "Prescription For The Happy Life," Dr. Jarvis told about his best friend dying of a massive cerebral hemorrhage and how he regretted not witnessing to him about Jesus Christ as the Savior of the world. He wrote this poem:

"Good Intentions"
by Dr. Charles Jarvis

Life's a trial and life's a worry
Life's a problem and life's a hurry
Life's a busy crowded way
Good intentions gone astray.

I had a friend the other day
I haven't now because he passed away.
I meant to write, to phone, to call
But he didn't hear from me at all.

I only hope that he can see
What his friendship meant to me
Life's a busy crowded way
Good intentions gone astray.

Remember, *life is so incredibly short!* Yesterday is gone. Tomorrow isn't guaranteed. Today is all you have to determine your destiny and legacy. It's what Cavett Robert taught me many years ago at that convention in Phoenix, Arizona. It's what Dr. Jarvis stressed in his poignant poem. And it's what I've tried to convey to you in this pithy book.

My hope is that these words will inspire you to be more intentional. My prayer is that you'll be self-motivated enough to fulfill your vast potential by acting today. God bless you in the pursuit and practice of these ten truths for making the most of your life.

"Intentions don't determine your destination, direction does. In order to go from where you are to where you want to be, it's going to require sacrifice to change your direction."

—ANDY STANLEY

TODAY'S THREE TIMELY QUESTIONS

"Most of our lives are crucified between
two thieves, yesterday and tomorrow.
We never live today. But the time
to live is now. It is today."

—W. OSCAR THOMPSON

You should ask these three timely questions for greater intentionality:

- **What will I *do* today?**

- **What have I *done* today?**

- **What will I keep *doing* tomorrow?**

The first question is about **priorities** and should be asked at the beginning of today. This is a written list of your (1) scheduled appointments and (2) other activities that can be done any time throughout the day. Alert—you'll probably have to adjust to some unplanned priorities.

The second question is about **performance** and should be asked at the end of today. These are the priorities you were able to implement. Transfer any unaccomplished priorities to a future date and eventually they'll either be completed or deleted because they're no longer important.

The third question is about **persistence** and should be asked at the end of today as well. Whatever you did successfully today, keep doing it. Conversely, whatever you did unsuccessfully today, quit doing it or change your approach and try to succeed tomorrow.

There's a place called The Intentional Growth Center at Lake Junaluska, North Carolina in the mountains of western North Carolina. Judy and I have run by this facility many times over the years, but we have no idea what this organization does. However, isn't it an intriguing concept?

If you don't have an intentional growth center in your life, why not create one? Nothing will make you more on-purpose than a commitment to betterment in your faith, with your loved ones and mentors, in your community and career, and with your money and health. Start TODAY by asking these three timely questions in the important areas of your life and make it a daily habit.

ACTION PLAN

"The deepest knowing comes only in doing."
—OS GUINNESS, *TIME FOR TRUTH*

A friend once asked me to summarize what I do for a living in one sentence. My reply: "I tell people things they already know and haven't done!" No doubt you probably know a lot of what you've just read, but perhaps you're now ready to act on what you know and haven't done. If so, please complete your action plan TODAY. It will help you cross *The Greatest Gap In Life* ©—the one between knowing and doing!

I hereby pledge to be more intentional in the following areas of my life by doing:

Time _____

God _____

Family _____

Friends _____

Master Mentors _____

Community _____

Career _____

Money _____

Serenity/Healthiness _____

Legacy _____

Signature _____ Date _____ Place _____

DICK BIGGS BIO

Dick Biggs is "The A-Line-Ment Specialist" because he works with organizations to boost *bottom-line* profits and better the *top line*— people and their productivity. He does so as a keynote speaker, seminar leader and author on leadership, mentoring, teamwork and work/life balance.

Dick has traveled to all fifty states and several foreign nations to serve a diverse group of clients—Fortune 500 companies, small businesses, government agencies, trade associations, educational institutions and nonprofits. Since 1990, his biggest client has been a legendary insurance and financial services company, where he has delivered hundreds of customized leadership programs to thousands of their agents.

He's the author of four other books: *Burn Brightly Without Burning Out; If Life Is A Balancing Act, Why Am I So Darn Clumsy; Wisdom Gold* and *Leading Your Insurance Agency To Greatness* with coauthor Scott Foster. He's also the creator of *Maximize Your Moments With The Masters*, a yearlong mentoring program.

Prior to starting his business in 1982, Dick was a sports-writing intern for the *Atlanta Constitution* and staff writer for the Associated Press. He also spent thirteen years in sales and sales management and graduated at the top of his class at Sales Training, Inc.

A Marine sergeant, Dick served as a security guard at the American embassies in Warsaw, Poland and Rome, Italy. After completing seven marathons, thirteen half-marathons, thirty Peachtree Road

Races and numerous other races, Dick now runs about fifteen miles every week and is a cofounder of the Chattahoochee Road Runners—Georgia's second-largest running club.

In addition, Dick is a past president of the National Speakers Association-Georgia and a recipient of the Kay Herman Legacy Award, this chapter's highest honor.

Dick is married to Judy and they reside on Lake Lanier north of Atlanta. They have two grown daughters (Rebecca and Tara), a son-in-law (Bo) and fifteen-year-old grandson (Jackson). Dick and Judy are small-group leaders at their church. Dick mentored Scotty Cole from the first grade through his high school graduation in 2012. Dick loves to solve crossword puzzles, play Scrabble, read, travel, root for the Georgia Bulldogs and listen to harmonious doo-wop oldies.

Dick is president of Biggs Optimal Living Dynamics (BOLD!) based at 9615 Settlers Lane, Gainesville, Georgia 30506. He can be contacted at 770-886-3035 or dickbiggs@att.net. His website is: www.biggspeaks.com

Made in the USA
Charleston, SC
01 December 2016